# My
# Next
# Shot
# Goes
# In!

# My Next Shot Goes In!

## Ten Sacred Characteristics of NBA Players That Lead to Success

*[signature]*

### Mike "Stinger" Glenn

My Next Shot Goes In!
Mike "Stinger" Glenn

ISBN: 978-0-9913609-0-1

Printed in the United States of America

First Printing                              1 2 2 7 1 3

This paper meets the requirements of ANSI/NISO Z39.48-1992 (Permanence of Paper)

Cover art courtesy of Reggie Gillumo, artgillumo@yahoo.com. NBA action photos courtesy of Getty Images as attributed.

# Contents

Mike Glenn, Walt Frazier, and Corky Abrams
in the Locker Room at Southern Illinois University

# Foreword

*I* can recall very vividly meeting Mike at S.I.U. I was impressed by his knowledge of the game and tenacious work ethic. He was very gregarious and liked by all.

We find it uncanny how our lives have so many similarities. Both having Georgia roots, then both attending S.I.U., playing for the Knicks and broadcasting.

Mike Glenn has taken on the admirable challenge of analyzing successful characteristics of NBA players and sharing them with everyone. He presents them in an intellectual yet engaging way. We all can benefit by reflecting on these traits and incorporating them into our daily activities. The object is not to make all of the readers NBA players or even basketball players: it is to encourage everyone to increase his or her best effort and reach the highest goal possible with the best attitude possible. He also did a good job of encouraging spiritual values as a part of the striving for success. His book leads all of us to re-assess our strategic use of our minds and bodies. The quotes that he chose at the end of each chapter helped to clarify the main point of each chapter and connected the perspectives of NBA players to successful people in diverse walks of life.

I have appreciated Stinger's approach to basketball and life. He played the game with precision and shared his success with others. There have not been many who could shoot the ball as well as he did. I have always been a fan of his basketball camp for Deaf and Hard of Hearing athletes. The Citizenship award that he won from the NBA was well deserved.

*My Next Shot Goes In* is a very good book that goes beyond the parameters of sports. It will help anyone who takes time to absorb the timeless messages. I see it as a personal development as much for a CEO as an aspiring basketball player. I wish you the reader and Stinger much success.

— Walt Frazier

# Acknowledgments

Like most books, this one has developed from many people and groups who have influenced my life. Their lessons, examples, inspiration, and encouragement have enriched me and my writing in countless ways. They cannot be individually thanked or repaid, but I sincerely acknowledge their contributions by "paying it forward" to others who don't know them nor share their lives.

I am thankful for my son, Michael Justin Glenn, and his contributions to this book. One of the reasons I wrote it was to leave a legacy to him. This book would serve as a literal, spiritual, and educational inspiration handed down to me from my parents and through me to Michael.

When he agreed to record my hand-written book on the computer, I was encouraged to better present these sacred characteristics to our readers. I dictated the entire book to him and proudly watched him fill the pages with messages that would empower readers.

My very good friend, Mrs. Virginia Meldrum, graciously edited these lessons and supplied me with ideas, suggestions, and corrections. In the middle of her personal challenges and demands of her attention and energy, she dug deep into her treasure chest of resolve, love of books, and respect for our friendship and project, and gave me brilliant adjustments.

Thanks also to Reginald Gillumo for sharing his expertise and providing the cover artwork and to the NBA for providing photographs.

# Introduction

**W**elcome to a great adventure! You are the right person, this is the right time, and you have chosen the right book to help you create and follow your unique path to a more successful and satisfying life. Ideas and opportunities have knocked upon your door because you have been chosen to receive them. Your goal is to maximize the experience of being alive. You will take risks because you are capable of many things. You will claim and own your circumstances and obstacles because they were either created by you or put there for you. Acceptance of these tenets will lead to your progress and ultimately to your evolution as a fully developed builder of a successful life. There are great rewards on the other side of your challenges. Keep going!

Thanks for allowing me to share some thoughts and experiences from NBA players and others that can lead you to daily success. My goal is to help you advance beyond the circumscribed place that someone has provided for you. May you start an adventurous journey that creates or reveals a better destiny than you imagined.

To start: Release the requirement of proceeding only when the image of a goal is in view. Give up the need to see your entire path from start to finish. Live life's adventure wholeheartedly. Discover the crooked paths as well as the multitude of goals, big and small. Accept the discomfort, obstacles, doubts, and insecurities as inevitable parts of the journey. Nurture the budding enthusiasm you feel when passing through uncharted paths. Accept guidance and direction from unpredictable and unusual sources. Do not be distracted by the seduction of apparent security elsewhere. Do not wait for validation by friends, family, or associates. Become the leader, magician, and genius who directs your life. The quality of your thoughts and the perseverance of your spirit will determine your destiny. Start projects, develop skills, consult with yourself, and celebrate your emergence from mediocrity to greatness!

Following are ten characteristics that are integral parts of an NBA player's personality. Most players are consciously aware of these traits; others develop them without analyzing their wisdom. The NBA culture leads players to make conditioned responses that lead to success. Personalize and apply these characteristics and responses to the field of your choice. My next shot goes in. How about yours?

Oscar Robertson

# *1*

## *Accept the Challenge*

*T*o build a successful life, accept the challenge to become your own head coach, trainer, and cheerleader. It is your privilege and responsibility to create an exceptional life because you are an exceptional person - literally, "One of a kind."

Oscar Robertson advised, "The harder you work to improve your skills, the more you'll enjoy the process. Even if you never play in organized competition, take pride in the fact that you took up the challenge to make a better player of yourself. It will serve you well in life."

Robertson pointed out that we would enjoy the process of developing our skills by working diligently. He reminded us to appreciate the courage necessary to challenge ourselves even without reaching a goal. Robertson saw a lesson for success in the struggle to improve - its byproducts of developed skills, increased energy, and confident character would create a better person. Use your imagination to create mental games that occupy your mind while you work to improve your skills. Enjoy your improvement and the imaginary victories that energize your activities.

In order to more fully enjoy the process of improving, Robertson suggests that you pull yourself beyond your comfort level. There you'll find progressive actions joyous. Direct the energy of your mind, body, and spirit to expanding your abilities and elevating your skills. Fully immerse yourself in developing your talents whatever they are. Hold nothing back; commit to letting your experiences define your days and your character.

Working to improve yourself does not have to make sense to anyone but you. Enjoy unfolding the unique mysteries of your life. Each action that you take will have its own benefit. Perhaps the benefit will be different than the one you had hoped for. You may not reach the desired destination, but you can be proud of your dedicated efforts. No one can ever take away the positive effects that were created—they become a part of you.

The risk of failure may make you hesitant to accept big challenges. Michael Jordan addressed that concern when he said, "I can accept failure; everybody fails at something, but I can't accept not trying." Jordan is pointing out the importance of accepting challenges regardless of the risks and occurrences of failure. He wants us to realize that the greatest failure is a refusal to try. As a matter of fact, there are no accomplishments without obstacles and few accomplishments without risks of some kind.

Our goal is to live an optimal life without settling for mediocrity. To reach that goal, you must attempt more than others. My mother taught all her children and students to follow Ralph Waldo Emerson's advice, "Go not where the path may lead; go instead where there is no path and leave a trail." You must accept risks because you are capable of many things beyond your current skill levels. Seeking comfort, safety, and reassurance will limit your progression and evolution.

Last, you must accept challenges to aid in the development of your abilities and talents. Don't accept "It can't be done; ask "How can I do it?"

So, go ahead and stretch yourself through active experiences. Go beyond your expectations by accepting the risk of embarrassment and blame. Strive to move forward in the direction of your choice. Improve for the sake of improving. Go where others are reluctant to go. Cross more lines, dare more, proclaim more, live more, and challenge more limits. You can handle more, do more, and be more than you've ever imagined. Use obstacles for steppingstones, circumstances for dares, and challenges for motivators to change your life to your advantage.

> "Instead of fighting and resisting my obstacles, perhaps I should treat them as new sources of information for me. Maybe there is a way to use my mind, body, and emotional life to create new possibilities."
>
> – Rudy Reyes

> "There is no passion to be found playing small- in settling for a life that is less than the one you are capable of living."
>
> – Nelson Mandela

> "Always doing what is pleasurable and/or easy to do sets one up for a weak foundation in life. For there is nothing special about easy. It is the conquering of the difficult that makes one special and even appreciated."
>
> – KRS-One

> "For everything that has been hard, I've had 25 positive things come from it."
>
> – Andy Roddick

Michael Jordan

Bill Bradley

# 2

## *Focus Is Key*

*T*hought / attention / concentration / focus / meditation are the keys to improvement. Bill Bradley is a former United States senator, a Rhodes Scholar, a college professor, and a New York Knicks forward. As a basketball player, he practiced so much that he developed what he called "a sense of where you are." He could start shooting the ball before looking at the basket because he had developed a sense of the basket's location in relation to his place on the court. Bradley focused intensely on making at least 10 of 13 shots from various locations on the court. When he had perfected the basketball player's version of a GPS system, he wrote the book titled "A Sense of Where You Are."

The ultimate goal of Bradley and other NBA players was to enter a sort of hypnotic state where the rim expanded, the ball shot itself, and almost every shot went in the basket. It was like being in the "Land of Oz" and the shooter was the wizard. Players strived to reach and to remain in this active state of meditation as long as possible. That state of euphoria was never attained easily nor often. Most players are not sure how they got there, but they know some of the prerequisites.

To reach this basketball heaven, you have to go through a process of being mentally reborn. It requires filling long hours in the gym with deliberate shooting practice. Your intent for each individual shot must be undivided. It demands focusing your thoughts to the 5th power. Players learn that they must turn the full purpose and power of their minds onto their activity. They realize that merely going through the motions to pass time or to fill a quota is squandering power. Players invest 100% into these activities because the ballers with the best use of the power of the mind realize the greatest success, enter the Land of Oz, and experience a rebirth through muscle memory.

Level One is thinking possibility thoughts and identifying the attraction and thrill of the ball going through the hoop. The first step is to create an atmosphere of fun; that seems to be the birthplace of possibility thoughts. At the youngest age, fun through participation, encouragement, and camaraderie is more important than competition. Give those emerging positive thoughts a good nurturing environment so they can grow and develop. The repetition of good thoughts creates energy for action and often directs our activities toward positive goals.

Adults can often make better choices of the thoughts they choose to hold onto when they realize that thoughts are causes, and each cause has an effect. You always have control over the thoughts that take up residence in your mind. Some may visit without your permission, but only you can invite them to stay. Don't let others decide for you which thoughts win the nesting environment of your brain and soul. No talk show, no evening news, no entertainer, no author, no employer, no minister, and not even a pope should be able to take away your ability to think for yourself. Your brain contains approximately 100 billion nerve cells. Feed them only the best progressive thoughts you can imagine.

Let your dreams and imagination soar without the weight of beliefs in probabilities.

On Level 2, attention takes priority. Attention is a form of sustaining the thrill and attraction of your beneficial thoughts—to hold on to them. Fleeting thoughts can have no long lasting effects. In order to make changes, it becomes necessary to eliminate distractions and random thoughts. This is why some parents, coaches, preachers, and teachers tend to shout. They are trying to hold your attention. Place your attention squarely on the mission in front of you and empower your efforts.

Often, even with adults, we seek to increase attention by actively eliminating distractions. Red Holtzman, legendary championship coach of the New York Knicks, often covered the windows of our practice facilities. He didn't want anyone looking out or anyone looking in. He did this at the training facilities at Monmouth College in New Jersey and at our practice sites at local colleges in Queens, New York. This was during the era when Jordache and Gloria Vanderbilt jeans were fashionable. The co-eds of those campuses wore their jeans well. You might even say that they maximized their potential. Red Holtzman was a great coach for more than his knowledge of X's and O's—he knew how to keep his players' attention focused on basketball.

Paying attention must be an active conscious effort. The more attention you bring to anything, the more interesting it becomes. Find ways and reasons to increase your attention to your goals while ignoring or eliminating the distractions around you. Countless things compete for your attention, but you can decide which things are worthy of your time and energy.

Level Three is concentration. It is best defined by Webster's College Dictionary as the process of increasing the strength, density, or intensity of something or a closed or fixed attention. Concentration is a way of perfecting a process or mastering its mechanics. In basketball and in life, rituals are often repeated as a sort of warm-up or advance preparation before a shot is taken.

Concentration is an intense mental process that can utilize visualization, but it must include repetition. You learn to improve your concentration by focusing your full attention on the details of all aspects of your practice. As you learn to shoot or to do anything else, treat it as if it is the only thing in the world that matters to you.

Ted Williams, recognized as one of the greatest players in baseball history, was considered a gifted athlete with innate abilities. He considered that thought a "lot of bull." He declared "the reason I saw things was that I was so intense." Williams's boyhood friend said, "His whole life was hitting the ball."

Intense concentration can make the difference between being good and being great.

Level Four is focus. Here you add your plan, expectations, purpose, and intent. You plan what, when, where, and how you will practice. You expect consistent improvement in your daily performance. Your purpose is to become exceptionally good. Your intent is to maximize your abilities. Focus becomes your quest for perfection which leads you to believe that every shot is going in the basket. That mindset requires a goal-oriented approach. With focus, practice becomes more deliberate than random and positive results increase markedly.

A Swedish psychologist, Anders Ericsson, organized a research army of scientists who spent more than thirty years analyzing relationships between talent, the brain, and achievements. They concluded that deliberate practice "is shown to induce physiological strain which causes biochemical changes that stimulate growth and transformation of cells, which in turn leads to associated adaptations of physiological systems and the brain."

In simpler words, they found that an imperfect shooting technique or other activity can be self-corrected through deliberate practice. Ericsson clarified deliberate practice as a very special form of activity. It differs from mere experience and mindless drills by including a repeated attempt to reach beyond one's current level. In short, it requires focus.

To focus properly, you need to put aside ego, accomplishments, anxieties, and aspirations. You must completely engage in the process at hand in the present moment. You will experience a form of connection and a form of freedom. Restrictions are released and energy is directed. New standards are established as you become the activity and the activity becomes you.

Focus completely and finish successfully.

Level Five is meditation—the highest use of your mind. Some people meditate instinctively; for others it is a learned activity. This level of thinking requires a release of your objectives and techniques to a stillness that is a cosmic form of listening. Meditation allows us to take in information from universal and unknown sources, often referred to as God. It connects us to an infinite power that is willing to give of itself to us. This process requires you to submit your concentrated desires to the greater power of the universe.

The merger of wills can only be accomplished through a lofty stillness. As Eckhart Tolle said, "Stillness is the language God speaks, and everything else is a bad translation."

There are great men and women in our history who have successfully merged much of their will with the universe's will. As a result, they spoke and acted with timeless wisdom. They were sometimes called mystics, not because they were mysterious, because they had an inner sense and understanding of the progressive and evolving universe. They seemed to perceive truth intuitively without entangling themselves in the common perceptions and limiting beliefs of their time. People like Akhenaton, Frederick Douglass, Harriet Tubman, Sojourner Truth, Lucy Stone, Henry David Thoreau, Malcolm X, Howard Thurman, Mohandas Gandhi, and Martin Luther King Jr learned through a spiritual process—they were taught by God.

So, create and follow your unique path to greatness. Dwell on the highest mountain peaks of your mind. Live in the spirit that is revealed to you. Master your body's potential. You will conceive and comprehend great thoughts; your mind and body will develop strength and power; and your skills and achievements will multiply. You will succeed far beyond your present dreams. Your shots will go in the basket of life.

"Tell your mind what to think."

– Les Brown

"First, you must be quiet within yourself. You must not be confused by outward appearance. Never become disturbed by effects. They didn't make themselves and have no intelligence to contradict you."

– Ernest Holmes

"The student who learns that power comes from within, that he is weak only because he has depended on help from outside, and who unhesitantly throws himself on his own thoughts, instantly rights himself, stands erect, assumes a dominant attitude, and works miracles."

– Charles Haanel

"Man is made or unmade by himself; in the armory of thought he forges his weapons by which he destroys himself; he also fashions the tools with which he builds for himself heavenly mansions of joy and strength and peace."

– James Allen

Larry Bird

# 3

## Make Your Thoughts As Big As Your Dreams

**M**any people spend so much of their mental energy and powers of imagination on their long term goals and dreams that they often fail to place significant emphasis on the day to day building block activities that make dreams a reality. All endeavors have fundamentals that serve as the foundations of higher success. You must learn to place value on the incremental steps that allow you to raise your level of competence. Build the small thoughts so completely that they become ingrained in your subconscious as part of your character. Crowd your mind and imagination with so many positive thoughts and images that there is little room or time for any other focus. Treasure the small basic steps that lead to victory.

In order to increase the effectiveness of your daily activities, envision yourself practicing ideal activities perfectly. You should always work on skills that produce your desired results. Make a commitment for excellence in these drills. In your mind make each action significant and important. Constantly contrast the quality of your work against the ideals that you have established. See each day as a complete journey with a destination of its own. Demand excellence and see yourself as a daily champion of details. As you put together successful days, they will turn into weeks and months full of concentrated efforts. Automatically, you will move closer to your goals and create the star that you have imagined.

Larry Bird said, "One reason I was able to do well was that I mastered the fundamentals." Magic Johnson added, "I told myself at an early age that I could never make enough passes in drills or at practice." Michael Jordan concluded, "Everything I did, everything I achieved, can be traced back to the way I approached the fundamentals and how I applied them to my abilities." These and other NBA stars recognized the need to put mental and physical power into every daily empowerment session. They built their success on the daily expansion of their skills.

Take the steps, regardless of the size and number, that enrich your life and develop your skills. Victories are won by consistently doing small fundamental things correctly. When we stop taking those small steps, for any reason, we stop our progress and abort our potential. You cannot foresee the results of even the most trivial acts. You don't know what forces you can set into motion to work on your behalf. Much may depend on committing yourself to excellence and to paying attention to your small acts. Opening the door of opportunity and achieving greatness begins with mastering the fundamentals. The mental energy that you apply to your actions impacts the effects of those actions in the short and long term. Add value to yourself daily by making small steps into excellence.

"Be true to yourself, help others, make every day your masterpiece, make friendship a fine art, drink deeply from good books - especially the Bible, build a shelter against a rainy day, give thanks for your blessings, and pray for guidance every day."

– John Wooden

"Decide what you want to do in life and put one foot ahead of the other."

– Bill Clinton

"Treat every second as holy...Whether it appears on the surface to be pedestrian or prestigious, tedious or tremendous, every moment must be infused with love and hard work.
There is simply no other way to find long term success in this world."

– Russell Simmons

"Try to do little things in an extraordinary way. ... Always center your whole mind on whatever you may be doing, however small or seemingly unimportant it may be."

– Paramahansa Yogananda

"Every day it's up to you to convert the soul's energy into the meaning of your life."

– Deepak Chopra

Magic Johnson

Kareem Abdul-Jabbar and Magic Johnson

# 4

## Enjoy the Journey

**K**areem Abdul-Jabbar was joined on the Los Angeles Lakers by rookie Earvin "Magic" Johnson. Abdul-Jabbar had already won several NBA awards including MVP, Rookie of the Year, and NBA champion. After securing the first victory of that season with a game-winning sky hook, Abdul-Jabbar was hugged aggressively and almost attacked by the excited rookie named Johnson. Abdul-Jabbar reasoned that there were 81 more games before the playoffs so he didn't feel much excitement. He later stated that Magic made him realize—and remember—that they were having fun.

Does someone have to remind you that you are having fun? Some people spend their whole lives waiting for the happiness that must surely be around the corner. They wait for graduations, for satisfactory employment, for marriage, for children, and for retirement. They wait for happiness that they may never see. They fail to live in the present because they are always preparing to live in the future.

This is your day, your time, and your moment. You have arrived. You are here, so why should you wait to go somewhere else? Where is the joy? Where are you going to find it? Bring your own joy with you wherever you go and whatever you do. Maximize the experience of being alive!

Live, enjoy, and celebrate your life as it is. Comparing yourself to others and measuring yourself against them is inaccurate and irrelevant. Even measuring yourself against your expectations and former achievements can retard, frustrate, and stop your progress. Stretch, grow, expand, and enjoy without self-created anxiety. Celebrate and appreciate your place, accomplishments, relationships, and associations throughout each day.

Your journey is yours and yours alone. No one can adequately share or understand the depths of your passions. Your vision and purpose were given to you alone. You may need to travel to sacred and quiet places without a companion to discover them. These solo flights on mental, physical, emotional, or spiritual journeys are part of the sometimes uncomfortable routes that you must travel to activate your potential and reach your destiny.

We confuse our time on earth with obsessions of where we are going and how we are looking. We stall our progress, evolution, and learning until we feel assured that we are going in the right direction to a place of our choice. Many of us are afraid of uncertainty despite the fact that it is always with us. Many wait for the perfect alignment of circumstances. We want first to be content, happy, and satisfied. We say we'll proceed with life's challenges as soon as we get our money, or something else, right.

Well, the perfect alignment will never come. We will never get it all together. We don't have to reach that favorable destination before we can start enjoying our journey. Growing, evolving, experiencing, and expressing shape our destination. We can only enjoy life when we admit and understand that we have no control over the future. We must loosen our fixation on a destination and let the journey unfold. Beauty, love, God, and happiness can only be experienced, observed, and appreciated. Our futile attempts to corner, capture, and domesticate these elusive spirits will only frustrate and misguide us.

Experience each moment as new and fresh. Expose yourself to criticism and judgment. There is no reason to hold back and restrict yourself. Go beyond activities that are safe and predictable. Become an adventurer. Smile, laugh, and have a good time on the journey. Find a way to enjoy what life has to offer, and you will discover more life to enjoy. Be kind, considerate, thoughtful, and helpful. Learn the benefits of acting in the presence of uncertainty. We are led to understand that we can never foresee the results of our actions. Even when the actions appear trivial, any action may open the door of growth, joy, and development. We may even intersect with a destiny-defining moment. Allow divine guidance to present itself.

Open your mind and appreciate everything. Let go of all your resentments and resistance to life. Feel and show abundant gratitude. This allows you to fully engage in the present and to absorb the beauty of the moment. It is more important to be grateful than to be hopeful. Hope's tendency to look ahead can rob you of present joy. Gratitude celebrates the present, allowing each moment to be filled with joy. Gratitude is a realization, an appreciation, and an expression of love. The release of this form of joy allows even more joy to enter into your consciousness. Gratitude enlivens and enriches your journey.

The mystery of life is incomprehensible; live it!

"Celebrate life no matter what your situation is."
– Rob Reiner

"Be patient toward all that is unresolved in your heart and try to love the questions themselves."
– Rainer Rilke

"Life is an exciting adventure or nothing at all."
– Helen Keller

"Ingratitude is one of the greatest of all sins."
– Dr. Martin Luther King Jr.

Karl Malone

# 5

## Take Pride in Your Body and Invest in Yourself

**K**arl Malone and Kevin Willis, among others, loved their bodies. They worked hard all year long to perfect them and to maintain them. They not only developed confidence and stamina; they took pride in the constant elevation of their physical stature. One of Malone's teammates, Greg Ostertag, supposedly once said "If we worked as hard as Karl, we would all be stars." The investments made by Willis and Malone are still paying dividends. They both look like competitive bodybuilders or current professional NBA players despite having retired many years ago.

We all should invest in ourselves as they do. The very best thing you can do for the whole world is to make the most of yourself regardless of your circumstances. Take yourself seriously. Guide and direct your life. Tell your mind what to think, your body what to do, your mouth what foods to eat, yourself which books to read and what music and art to appreciate. Be a creator of your destiny and your reality by making fruitful investments in yourself. Consciously or not, you will invest your concentrated energy and resources in something. Why not invest in yourself and your development? Love yourself enough to devote time and energy on you. If you love yourself enough, you will be willing to suffer to make a more loveable you. The desire and intention to evolve and become what you can be has to be very important. Invest in your history, your progression, and your health. Feed your soul seeds that produce the harvest you desire. You are the only one who can do what must be done in those areas.

Investing in yourself is a process of expanding your influence, increasing your abilities, growing your confidence, empowering your will and resolve, and developing your potential. The first step is to increase your awareness of your surroundings. Become present! Notice and choose your thoughts.

Your goal is to strengthen the causes that sustain and define you. Every cause has an effect. Every thought, word, and deed triggers a reaction in the universe. You never know what the ripple effect will be of even your smallest actions. Strengthen your actions and make sure they are sanctioned by the power of your thoughts and desires.

Investing in yourself is an active pursuit of all those things that lead to your evolution. That pursuit compels us to take responsibility for our lives and circumstances. It suggests that we can influence our environment and overcome feelings of fear, anxiety, and other discomforts. Go ahead and commit to empowering yourself, spiritually, mentally, nutritionally, physically, and emotionally. Commit to an active life of continual growth and development. Release from your mind all statistics, habits, beliefs, restrictions, and limitations that suggest mediocre performance. Protect your drive, energy, passion, and progress. You can do more than you imagine. Become unstoppable!

Taking pride in yourself and your body starts with realizing two things: (1) you are a part of the energy and intelligence that created the universe, and (2) that intelligence is a part of you. In short, you are an individualized expression of God. You can, therefore, create your reality. It need not coincide with anyone else's reality or beliefs. Take pride in your responsibility to love and develop yourself before you seek to help others. As a result, your gifts will be valued more highly and your significance will be enhanced. People will naturally discount your thoughts, words, and ideas until they see clear evidence that you have loved yourself enough to achieve tangible results.

Remember also to invest in your intellectual growth. Your physical body is not the only point of interest; expand your mental abilities because all progress comes from intelligence. Using your intelligence wisely provides the answers to every question and the solutions to all problems. Read, reflect, and observe to expand your awareness and knowledge. Read about successful people that you would like to emulate. Analyze and discuss the characteristics and thoughts that propelled them to success. Take notes from the books you read so that you can go back to the most inspiring aspects of your heroes. Start a book collection and surround yourself with stories that motivate you.

Say "Yes!" to anything that leads to your growth, development, and evolution. Say "No!" to all people who depress or discourage you in any way. Let no obligation to others prevent you from making the most of yourself. Anyone who encourages you to do less or to become less than your best is neither a true nor a wise friend. Instead of lowering your expectations and quality of work, raise them through increased desire, passion, and love. Be cautious when exchanging words, thoughts, and goals with people who do not believe in you and your potential. Their limited views, beliefs, and experiences can deflate your ambition and depress your initiative. They consciously or unconsciously discredit your accomplishments and minimize your abilities. Do not empower them or their views with agreement nor resentment. Reserve your energy for more worthy endeavors like investing in yourself.

I once heard one of my favorite musicians, the late Freddie Hubbard, say he wished he could play like Wynton Marsalis. As I see the comparison, Hubbard played the trumpet as well as anyone of his era including Wynton Marsalis. Hubbard's style and training may have been different but never inferior to anyone's. I wondered if the Indiana icon, Hubbard, may have had less pride in himself than Marsalis, the New Orleans native and curator and custodian of jazz history. I guess in the final analysis, Hubbard had enough generosity to admire Marsalis and enough pride in himself to become one of the best musical masters in American history.

"Low self-esteem repels; confidence and self-sufficiency attract."
– Robert Greene

"The best investment you can make is in yourself."
– Warren Buffett

"Most people search high and wide for the key to success. If they only knew the key to their dreams lies within."
– Dr. George Washington Carver

"Most people fail because their visions of themselves are too small."
– Les Brown

"It is your job to train and invest in yourself."
– Reid Hoffman

Kevin Willis

George Gervin

# 6

## Build Your Strengths;
## Defend Your Weaknesses

**M**ost uninformed people will advise you to reach higher levels of success by working on your weaknesses. NBA players have a different, more effective strategy. They build their strengths and display them as often as possible atop mountains and defend their deficiencies in the valleys of seclusion and subterfuge.

Coaches look for players who excel at specific aspects of the game. A player's best skill becomes his handle. Coaches and teammates utilize him and recognize him by his handle. NBA scoring champ George Gervin yelled at his young teammate, Mike Mitchell, "Stop playing defense!" Mitchell, also a scorer, had picked up two early fouls by extending himself on the defensive end. Because of the fouls, he was forced to the bench. His time, energy, and talent would have been better served by competing through his strength, offense.

Everyone has special gifts and talents. Your job is to discover, nurture, utilize, and magnify yours. Your identity should be created and communicated through your strengths. By magnificently applying your physical, mental, and spiritual powers to your expertise, you will rise above normal and even rational levels. The forces created by passion, focus, and desire can be channeled through your talent and your gifted areas to produce abnormally high skill levels. Those highly developed skills will elevate you to new heights.

It will not take the people around you very long to recognize your strengths. These newly developed skills will become your light; let it shine. Your light, whatever it may be, should be central to everything you do. It should be placed in a visible position so it can provide guidance for others and illumination for your developed expressions. You must work with the best tools that God has given you. Analyze yourself and your marketable assets. Consult with friends and ask them what is special about you. The world is attracted to special, unique, productive, and attractive people.

You may have a unique way of presenting your contributions. You have only a limited time to captivate your audience. Master the art of minimizing the exposure of your deficiencies. When playing basketball, defensive players learn to give a quicker offensive player more distance or to force him toward a defensive teammate who can help. Players even learn to deny the entry pass to the gifted opponent. Weak defensive teams try to limit their liabilities by encouraging the offensive team to take quick, open shots from the perimeter. When the shot doesn't go in, they eagerly break back to their offensive end of the floor—their stronghold.

Show what you've developed and express your unique messages. Follow your passions and share their products. These are the advantages that will make you stand out from others. They will make your message more interesting and your skills more desirable. If you fail to do this, the world will likely miss noticing you and never realize what you had to offer. When you showcase your strengths, they overshadow your weaknesses.

"Stir up the gift of God which is within thee."
– Paul, the apostle

"Dyslexics often have a lot of success because they concentrate on areas they are good at."
– Sir Richard Branson

"Live only in your art."
– Ludwig van Beethoven

"Passion is not friendly. It is arrogant, superbly contemptuous of all that is not itself, and, as the very definition of passion implies the impulse of freedom, it has a mighty intimidating power. It contains a challenge. It contains an unspeakable hope."
– James Baldwin

Mike "Stinger" Glenn

Carmelo Anthony and Mike Woodson

# 7

## *Never Blame; Always Build*

If an NBA player misses a last second shot that would have won the game, pro basketball players would not blame the individual for the loss. They would say, "It's a team game that is 48 minutes long; that one shot didn't beat us. Maybe we could have made more shots earlier or not committed so many turnovers to help decide the outcome." Instead of blaming their teammate, they would immediately start building for the next game. Adjustments and corrections would be the topic of discussion rather than blame.

The team needs the enthusiasm, strength, energy, and intelligence of all its members. Why would they blame anyone for a single moment of action? The player who missed the shot would feel ostracized and dejected. Blaming discourages, devalues, and defeats while it closes the mind to progressive ideas. Individuals should have a goal to inhale disappointment and pain and to exhale optimism and wellness. Instead of blaming darkness, each member should provide light. The mind must not be encouraged to look down; all players should radiate positivity. Besides, a failure can motivate changes and may become the beginning of a great success story.

Coach Mike Woodson of the New York Knicks has very little tolerance for players who take time to blame themselves or others. He has had explosive players on his teams like Jamal Crawford, Joe Johnson, J.R. Smith, Josh Smith, and Carmelo Anthony. These and other players can have bad first half shooting performances which would suggest to the average fan that they should not look for their shots in the second half. At halftime Coach Woodson demands, "Don't hang your head and feel bad about the way you played; get your head up and get it back in the second half."

In our society, many hold onto yesterday's losses or disappointments and look for a scapegoat to blame. All circumstances are to be used for your advancement. Why blame anyone? Our media looks for conflict and controversy to attract attention and to create conversation. When a single person is held up as the cause for defeat or victory, the team is left with the emotional baggage of their coverage. NBA players know that yesterday's baggage is too heavy to drag around in today's game. Clinging to resentment does not bolster progress; it retards it. Negative attitudes can cause thoughts of entitlement and lead to defense of egos. Thinking that someone owes you something will adversely affect relationships and throw everyone off track. Even if you have contributed mightily, rid yourself of the thought and the attitude that someone owes you payment of any kind.

Strengthen your gratitude; it is the antidote for entitlement. Avoid an ego-based personality. Your ego can lead you to make five costly mistakes:

(1) to search for security rather than growth,

(2) to make limiting assumptions,

(3) to reject change,

(4) to disconnect from challenges, and

(5) to become defensive rather than progressive.

In defending your ego, you lose sight of your empowering purpose. Look to bring your actions into alignment with your purpose. Get to the point where you are not disturbed by things such as unfavorable events, tough circumstances, and difficult conditions. You and your ego are much healthier when it does not control your life.

"Don't waste time calculating your chances of success and failure. Just fix your aim and begin."

– Guan Yin Tzu

"If you bring forth what is within you, it will save you. If you do not, it will destroy you."

– Gnostic Gospel of Thomas

"Performing on this level leaves little room for anything else."

– Mary J. Blige

"People who cling to their illusions find it difficult if not impossible to learn anything worth learning. A people under the necessity of creating themselves must examine everything and soak up learning the way roots soak up water."

– James Baldwin

Dr. J

Lou Hudson

# *8*

---

# *Build Good Relationships*

**B**uilding good relationships is essential to team success on the court and an important factor in creating individual success. Lou Hudson provided a great example of relationship building.

Here's how Lou did it. While the Atlanta Hawks were in pre-game warm-ups, he would go to Pete Maravich and say, "Pete, it's you and me today. We guards have to do it. My outside jumper is going down; let's look for each other." He would then make his way to Bill Bridges. "Bill, it's you and me tonight. We're going to have to do it. If you get the ball on the post or get an offensive rebound and you don't have a scoring option, look for me in the corner. I'll knock down the jumper and get you an assist." Next, he'd find Walt Bellamy. "Walt," he would suggest, "it's you and me tonight, Big Fella. Let's run the pick and roll. If both defenders come to me, I'll pass inside to you. If they leave me open, I'll knock down the jumper." Later Lou would go over to Jim Washington and say, "Jim, it's you and me tonight. These guys have a tough interior defense. Let's stay on opposite sides of the floor and stay wide. You can always look for me cross court, and I'll do the same." By time the game started, everyone from players to coaches and ball boys was on Lou's side. They saw him as someone who cared about them.

NBA players learn at an early age that no one is wise enough or talented enough to achieve success by himself. They realize that others with common interests can share the load, lighten the burden, and bring more joy to the process. They learn to trust, to help, and to appreciate their teammates. Professional players discover ways they can create an atmosphere to help them develop, prosper, and gain recognition. Forming good relationships builds successful individuals and teams, but how do they do that?

They use the power of praise and the effect of inclusion. Humans and most other living things crave attention and the energy it generates. We do all sorts of things to get attention: perform stunts, dress in certain fashions, participate in activities, speak loudly, create controversies, develop our bodies, eat certain foods, buy bricks inscribed with our names, adopt highways, drive expensive cars, create dramas, sing, act, excel, compete, shout, tweet, advertise, show and tell, donate, run marathons, endure surgery, and develop skills. By complimenting their teammates and fans, players learn to affect their behavior and to form positive relationships so that "me and them" become "us."

Paying astute compliments is powerful proof that one cares enough to pay attention. This cause usually encourages reciprocation and the effects can be greater than the cause. The results can bring mutual enjoyment and positively impact those who merely observed the interaction. The joy and response create a culture that empowers and defines the team.

The secret to building good relationships can work for everyone. You need to remember to give attention to your associates and neighbors. Look, listen, observe, compliment, and energize them. By sharing your positive spirit, you will delight others, create an inclusive culture, and empower yourself. None of your actions or speech should cause sadness, depression, offense, or pain. Always carry healing and compassionate words with you wherever you go and dispense them generously. Every word should convey hope, encouragement, and energy.

Learn to perceive the needs of your peers. Reassure the insecure, befriend the lonely, laugh with the comedian, praise the undervalued, listen to the talkative, believe in the doubtful, and motivate the uninspired. Imagine all the people who will look for ways to return your kindness! You and your team will thrive in the positive culture you helped to create.

"If you can lift people's spirits and they can lift yours, you can survive."

– Bobby Womack

"Every time you smile at someone, it is an action of love, a gift to that person, a beautiful thing."

– Mother Teresa

"I find the more acceptance and liking I feel toward this individual, the more I will be creating a relationship which he can use. By acceptance I mean a warm regard for him as a person of unconditional self worth - of value no matter what his condition, his behavior, or his feelings. … It means an acceptance of and regard for his attitudes of the moment, no matter how negative or positive."

– Carl Rogers

"The truly wise man or woman will recognize no one as an enemy."

– Ralph Waldo Trine

Terry Cummings

# 9

## *Faith*

**H**aving faith means believing that your next shot is going in and that you can win each game whether it's on the basketball court or in another part of life.

I once heard Jeff Teague of the Atlanta Hawks say in a post-game interview that he always has confidence in his team. He believed that they would win each game. All NBA players have a similar kind of faith. They don't necessarily believe they will win all their games, but they believe they will win that day's contest. Shooters believe their next shot will go in the basket. Rebounders believe they will get the next rebound. I once heard Coach Don Nelson tell Terry Cummings that he wanted him to get every rebound in that particular quarter because the Bucks had a small lineup on the court. Cummings confidently answered, "OK."

For the NBA player, faith begins with incremental steps of success. The accumulation of each successful endeavor is strengthened by the emotional responses that often follow. The player envisions the ball going in the basket often enough to believe it will happen upon demand. He practices concentration and focus enough that he can independently determine the outcome of an attempt regardless of the success or failure of the previous shots. Practice does make perfect in the player's mind and vision.

Atlanta Hawks' trainer Joe O'Toole once posed this question in a joking way, "If a player were to practice ten free throws and miss six, was he practicing to miss or practicing to make?" Former Rhodes Scholar and NBA star Tom McMillen reasoned that Joe had intent confused with results. O'Toole's question still makes me wonder about any free throw shooter who shoots less than 50% - perhaps that player has been practicing to miss.

The first step of faith is belief. It precedes your success as a shooter or anything else. Faith is a developed concept that is neither innate nor transferable. To acquire it, start with a strong base of desire and build a foundation of progressive successful steps. Constant affirmations reinforce developing confidence. Faith's potential has no limits.

Faith is tough to pin down. It is not rational, not based on statistics or projections, and does not respect class, culture, history, race, or educational institution. Faith is intangible, but real; invisible, but present. Evidence of its impact is debatable so the results are often credited to luck, natural ability, or good coaching. In spite of these mysteries, faith is very valuable because it connects its possessor to the infinite power and wisdom that created the universe.

To maximize the power of faith, one also has to acquire its cofactors: confidence and courage. All three are interdependent and practically identical. One cannot have confidence without faith. If one truly has confidence, courage must soon follow. We need a word that implies the essence of all three. Margaret Mitchell, author of *Gone with the Wind*, understood the need for such a word. She said she liked people with "gumption." That sounds good! You gotta have gumption.

So, go ahead. Develop gumption and make daily declarations of faith. Determine to proceed even without tangible assurance, physical evidence, or comforting support. Realize that faith is not God working for you; it is God working through you. Understand that there are some things you cannot do: know all the details, see the full map of life, comprehend the entire message, or find all the dots to connect. Then be assured of this - you will prevail!

Morris Baxter, the host of Atlanta's WCLK morning radio show, shares his affirmation with the listening audience each morning. He says, "Something good is going to happen to you today." You declare out loud at least twice every day, "Something good is going to happen to me today." Believe those words and these faith-based thoughts and empower yourself to live beyond your present realities. Developing your faith guides your shots through the nets of life.

"The idea that faith has only to do with our religious experience is a mistake...faith is an affirmative mental approach to reality. Those who have great faith have great power."

– Ernest Holmes

"The man who fears something is already suffering from what he fears."

– Michel de Montaigne

"You can start with nothing and do anything."

– Chris Gardner

"I know for a fact that you can start at the absolute bottom of an organization, even working for free if need be, and within a few years, find yourself running that same organization."

– Russell Simmons

"Faith, absolute dogmatic faith, is the only law of true success. When we recognize the fact that a man carries his success or his failure with him, and that it does not depend upon outside conditions, we will come into the possession of powers that will quickly change outside conditions into agencies that make for success."

– Ralph Waldo Trine

NCAA Tournament 1977 SIU vs. Wake Forest

# 10

## Let the Universe Handle the Details

S hortly after graduating from Southern Illinois University and being drafted by the Chicago Bulls, I was involved in a car accident that fractured my third cervical vertebra. In seconds, that crash took me from feeling like I had the world on a string to feeling that life had me by the tail. For the first time in my life, I was not sure if I would ever play basketball again. Doctors seemed unsure how, if, or when the vertebra would heal. They even mentioned the possibility of taking bone from my hip to stabilize my neck. Whoa! I was not thrilled with the risks of surgery - especially on my spine.

Until the crash, there were two career paths open to me—professional basketball and business. I had been chosen the number one academic All-American basketball player in the country, had earned a BA degree in Mathematics from Southern Illinois, and had been awarded a postgraduate scholarship from the Missouri Valley Conference. Deciding which path to take was hard. At that time, successful investment bankers and stockbrokers were making as much money annually as many NBA players, and they had the probability of much longer careers. No matter what I decided, step one was to heal my neck.

I decided to visit my aunt, Myrtis Pitts, who had received more than one healing based on her prayers and strong faith. At her home in Chicago, that lady looked me in the eye and asked me what I wanted to do. Right then and there I declared, "Aunt Myrtis, I want to play basketball." Without hesitation, she assured me that we should pray exactly for that and God surely would let me reach my desired goal. Aunt Myrtis had visited SIU to meet her sister (my mom) and to watch me play basketball. She knew that I was prepared for the NBA. Aunt Myrtis and I prayed together that I would be healed and would play in the NBA. She counseled me to relax and to focus on my healing and my basketball career. She also told me to let God handle all the details. Staying focused on doing my part in the healing and rehabilitation program enabled me to pass the physical exam two months later. My neck was healed and my ten-year NBA career started!

I learned a lesson that may benefit you. The future is unknown and unknowable. You can neither control nor predict the events of your life. Proceed in the presence of ambiguity, uncertainty, fear, and contradictions. Know that you can never get something for nothing, and you will never get nothing for something. Surrender to the unknown and invisible power of the universe. Its force is all powerful and everywhere. Its dimensions and characteristics are beyond our ability to comprehend, but we can tap into it to change our lives.

Farmers understand this power and process better than most people. They cultivate the soil with mineral nutrients and plant good seeds before turning responsibility for the crop to the forces of the universe. The harvest is produced in proportion to the power of the seeds and the nutrients in the soil. Likewise, you should enrich your mind with knowledge and plant good mental and spiritual seeds in order to yield the maximum results. All of the earth is alive, intelligent, progressive, and fertile. The spirit of the creator is in the mind and the atmosphere as well as in the soil.

Release your need to understand exactly how things develop. You can't always see how the pieces will fit together. Consider the possibility that everything is as it should be despite your negative feelings. Your limited and conditioned logic may be a barrier to your breakthrough. Expectations can be the mental controls limiting bigger possibilities that are not envisioned or planned by you.

Learn to function and to grow without attaching your efforts to a conclusion. Push through doubt and loneliness to get to the beginning of surrender to God, the place where miracles happen. You will notice your anxiety lessening. It is at this time that you make peace with the present, realizing that God is there and that his intent must ultimately prevail. Allow this greater force to participate freely. Something much bigger than you imagined can happen. Let the universe handle the details.

"Success isn't something you chase. It is something you have to put forth the effort for constantly. Then maybe it will come when you least expect it."

– Michael Jordan

"Faith is taking the first step even when you don't see the whole staircase."

– Dr. Martin Luther King Jr.

"Few men, however great their wisdom, are permitted to see the end from the beginning."

– Frederick Douglass

"Go confidently in the direction of your dreams. Live the life you've imagined."

– Henry David Thoreau

"Whenever you can approach all of your work with a smile and make no distinction between success and failure, the world is going to open up in front of you and allow you to have your pick of blessings."

– Russell Simmons

COLLEGE SPORTS INFORMATION DIRECTORS OF AMERICA

Proudly Salutes

**MIKE GLENN**   of   **Southern Illinois**

AS AN

Academic All-America Basketball Player

**UNIVERSITY DIVISION 1976**

President—College Sports
Information Directors of America

Chairman—CoSIDA Academic
All-America Basketball Committee

CO-SPONSORED BY THE SCHOOL CALENDAR COMPANY

COLLEGE SPORTS INFORMATION DIRECTORS OF AMERICA

Proudly Salutes

**MIKE GLENN, G**   of   **Southern Illinois**

AS AN

Academic All-America Basketball Player

**UNIVERSITY DIVISION 1977**

Bill Esposito
President—College Sports
Information Directors of America

CoSIDA

Chairman—CoSIDA Academic
All-America Basketball Committee

SPONSORED BY SCHOOL CALENDAR COMPANY

Mike Glenn was a two-time Academic All-American. In 1977 he was selected as the number one Academic All-American in Division 1

# Author's Note

T hank you for allowing me to share with you my thoughts and observations on maximizing your potential, purposefully building successes for yourself, and generously creating an atmosphere that enables others to succeed. Use this book to feed your ambition and determination. It can help you develop the courage to keep trying in the presence of doubts, fears, and uncertainty. Recognize your worth, your uniqueness, and your connection to infinite resources.

Always believe that your next shot at success goes in!

# About the Author

**M**ike Glenn played ten years in the NBA, a career that almost didn't begin when he broke his neck in a car accident shortly after graduation. His teammates gave him the nickname "Stinger" for shooting the ball so accurately that he "stung" the nets. He set numerous records for his field goal and free throw accuracy.

"Stinger" earned the NBA Walter P. Kennedy Citizenship Award, and the NBA Players' Association "Spirit of Love" Award. He was selected because of his community work and for starting the nation's first free basketball camp for deaf and hard of hearing athletes. This camp, now 34 years old, began as a dream when Mike discovered in junior high that deaf kids could not go to sports camps—because there were no sports camps for deaf kids. As a young teenager, he declared "When I grow up, I'm going to start a basketball camp for deaf kids." In college, Mike volunteered during the summer with his school's camp for deaf kids. His dedication was so strong that he turned down invitations to try out for both the Olympics and the Pan American Games because they would have taken him away from the camp and his studies.

Glenn graduated from Southern Illinois University with a mathematics degree. He was recognized with the #1 Vote for Academic All-American Basketball Player during his senior year. Glenn later took graduate business courses at Baruch College and Saint John's University.

Glenn collects rare books, papers, magazines, and other documents of American history. He has written four books utilizing his extensive library as an inspiration and a resource.

Glenn is currently an inspirational speaker and a television basketball analyst.

For more information please visit:

## www.mikeglenn.com

# References

Allen, James. *As a Man Thinketh*

Beckwith, Michael Bernard. *Lifevisioning: A Transformative Process for Activating Your Unique Gifts and Highest Potential*

Brown, Les. *Living Your Dreams*

Chopra, Deepak. *Reinventing The Body, Resurrecting The Soul: How to Create a New You*

Frame, Donald (translated by). *The Complete Essays of Montaigne*

Gardner, Chris. *Start Where You Are: Life Lessons in Getting from Where You Are to Where You Want to Be*

Holmes, Ernest. *The Science of Mind*

Jordan, Michael. *I Can't Accept Not Trying*

KRS ONE. *The Gospel of Hip Hop*

Reyes, Rudy. *Hero Living: Seven Strides to Awaken your Infinite Power*

Rogers, Carl R. *On Becoming a Person: A Therapist'sView Of Psychotherapy*

Simmons, Russell. *Super Rich: A Guide To Having It All*

Yogananda, Paramahansa. *Where There is Light: Insight and Inspiration for Meeting Life's Challenges*